THE ROYAL COMMISSION ON CRIMINAL JUSTICE

The Conduct of Police Interviews with Juveniles

by **Roger Evans**

LONDON: HMSO

CONTENTS

Acknowledgements

This research was funded by The Royal Commission on Criminal Justice. I am particularly grateful to Julie Vennard for her advice, support and very thorough and helpful comments on earlier drafts of this report.

The study would not have been possible without the co-operation and help of all the police officers involved. I would like to thank those officers in the Administration of Justice Department and tape libraries who worked so hard to provide me with copies of taped interviews.

I am also grateful to colleagues in The University of Birmingham. Professor Peg Piel generously gave me the benefit of her experience of running SPSS on an Apple Macintosh. My colleagues from the Law Faculty were helpful as always. Tim Moloney coded half the interviews and freely gave me the benefit of his ideas and observations. He also commented on drafts of the report as did Roger Leng who was particularly generous with his time. Andrew Sanders discussed various aspects of the study with me.

Ann Lane and Sue Gilbert of the Department of Social Policy and Social Work helped with transcribing the interviews and the research would not have been possible without the continuing support of the Department.

Dr Roger Evans
The University of Birmingham
April 1992.

INTRODUCTION

This study consists of an analysis of the factors associated with confessions and denials during police interviews with juveniles. It examines the interview process and the relationship of the content of interviews to police records of whether or not juveniles have confessed.

Softely et al (1980) suggest that the usefulness of a confession to the police depends on the strength of the other evidence. When other evidence is weak a confession enables the police to clear up crime which would otherwise remain unsolved, but when strong it merely serves to strengthen the prosecution case. The usefulness of a confession also depends on the stage in the investigative process when the interview takes place. Interviews often occur when all the other evidence has not been fully gathered. Obtaining a confession, at that point in time, may appear to be more important than in retrospect (Irving 1980). The police may therefore be motivated to obtain a confession even when subsequently it is found that there is strong evidence connecting the suspect to the crime.

There is general agreement that obtaining a confession is one of the most useful and the quickest route to clearing up crime (Mawby 1979, Morris 1980, McConville and Baldwin 1981, McConville et al 1991). Clear up rates are an important measure of police efficiency. As many juvenile crimes are 'minor' (Parker et al 1981, Evans and Ferguson 1991) clearing them up by obtaining confessions may be a relatively easy way of demonstrating efficiency. Obtaining a confession enables the police to avoid gathering other kinds of evidence, for example witness statements or forensic evidence, and also avoids unnecessary delays in disposing of juvenile cases so maximising any deterrent effect of the disposal. Beside a confession recognises the rightness of the investigating officer's case, the soundness of his judgement and serves to reinforce perceptions of his skills and credibility amongst his colleagues (Laurie 1970).

Whilst a confession is generally thought by police officers to be the sign of a 'good' interview, and by implication a 'good' interviewer (Moston et al 1992), interviews may also serve other purposes. They may help to solve other crimes, recover stolen goods, and exonerate the innocent (Baldwin and McConville 1980).

A signed confession is, of course, invaluable to the prosecution (Lewis 1976). It makes a guilty plea more likely and so simplifies proceedings and avoids the attendance of witnesses (Franklin 1970). Paradoxically, for as long as obtaining confessions remains so important in police work, magistrates or juries may feel that a charge unsupported by a confession is weaker than it really is. Confessions are not always necessary to the prosecution case because of the strength of other evidence (McConville and Baldwin 1981), and may be disputed at trial (Mitchell 1983, Vennard 1985), but the interrogation nonetheless remains the *central investigative strategy* of the police (McConville et al 1991).

This may go some way to explain the degree of professional and public anxiety expressed about police interview techniques. A key concern here is the degree to which the accused should be made a witting or unwitting instrument in their own conviction. *'Specifically the issue is to what extent the police may exploit the timidity, ignorance, lack of foresight and stupidity of the suspect in order to obtain a conviction'* (Morris 1980).

This issue is particularly important with respect to juveniles who may be thought to be vulnerable, by reason of their age, to the use of persuasive techniques by the police. This is recognised by the code of practice to the 1984 Police and Criminal Evidence Act which suggests that special care may be needed when interviewing this age group. PACE also states that an interview with a juvenile should be in the presence of an appropriate adult.

> *'It is important to bear in mind that, although juveniles or persons who are mentally disordered or mentally handicapped are often capable of providing reliable evidence, they may, without knowing or wishing to do so, be particularly prone in certain circumstances to providing information which is unreliable, misleading or self-incriminating. Special care should therefore always be exercised in questioning such a person, and the appropriate adult should be involved, if there is any doubt about a persons age, mental state or capacity. Because of the risk of unreliable evidence it is also important to obtain corroboration of any facts admitted whenever possible.'*
> (PACE Code of Practice 1991 Notes for guidance 11B)

A key question here is the extent to which the police attempt to, or are able to, establish the degree of understanding of juvenile suspects. It is not sufficient to assume that juveniles understand the implications of statements that they make in interviews.

The issue of the reliability of confession evidence is particularly important in the case of juveniles as the majority are now disposed of without a court appearance because of the increased use of police cautioning. The average cautioning rate for juvenile males has risen from 45 per cent in 1980 to 72 per cent in 1990 and that for females from 70 per cent to 85 per cent in the same period. Home Office guidance, in force at the time that the data for the present study was collected, states that a caution should only be given when the offender confesses. *'It is not sufficient that the juvenile should admit all or some of the facts: he must recognise his guilt'*. (Home Office Circular 14/85). Since a caution is a disposal for crime it is only appropriate to caution when the juvenile has in effect pleaded guilty. This circular has since been replaced with Home Office Circular 59/90 which advises that a caution will only be appropriate when a person makes a *'clear and reliable admission of the offence'*. If they deny intent, for instance, then this would not amount to a full admission.

The increased use of cautioning to divert juveniles from court may be considered the sign of a humane and progressive juvenile system but it also heralds a shift from 'judicial' to 'administrative' justice (Pratt 1986). Pratt argues that pre-court decisions are largely taken behind closed doors in contrast to the public arena of the court. As a result there has been a significant increase in the powers of the police, in conjunction with other agencies, to intervene in the lives of young people without direct public accountability or scrutiny. This is arguably one of the more dramatic and less visible changes in the criminal justice system in the last decade.

The background to the research

This study is an extension of an earlier piece of research which examines how the police arrive at decisions to caution, prosecute or take no further action with juvenile suspects (Evans and Ferguson 1991). The Evans and Ferguson (1991) research followed a sample of 367 juvenile cases through the pre-court decision making process from the point of arrest. The research was conducted in a single police force that had different types of inter-agency consultation processes, bureaux and panels, operating in different areas.

The research confirmed that police interrogations play a key role in the decision making process. There is a marked lack of attention on the part of researchers to the conduct of police interviews with juveniles but there are many readily identifiable differences between interrogations of juveniles and adults. One of the most obvious characteristics of juvenile cases, in contrast to adult cases, is that juveniles are rarely alone when involved in incidents leading to charges. This gives scope for playing juvenile codefendants off against each other in various ways. For example by pointing out discrepancies in their stories or telling suspects that their 'mates' have named them and are prepared to act as witnesses. Evans and

Ferguson (1991) report the apparent eagerness with which juveniles 'grass each other up' and it is not unknown for police officers to play the tape of a co-suspect to the suspect in order to encourage an admission.

Other issues which give rise to concern in the Evans and Ferguson (1991) research include that, in some cases, questioning had taken place prior to the formal interview at the scene of the crime or in the car travelling to the police station. Information obtained in this way, when suspects may not have been formally arrested or under caution, was used as the basis for subsequent formal interrogations.

Evans and Ferguson (1991) also found that juveniles suspected of criminal offences were routinely arrested and detained in the station despite the view that arrest is a coercive power which may cause distress (Royal Commission on Criminal Procedure 1981). Indeed the majority of the arresting officers that were interviewed acknowledged that a significant proportion of juveniles find arrest and detention a distressing and frightening experience. This may render suspects psychologically vulnerable prior to and during police interviews. Suspects may readily admit to offences in order to obtain as quick a release as possible from an uncomfortable situation.

There is little evidence from the Evans and Ferguson (1991) research that juveniles have routine access to legal advice prior to interviews and solicitors were present in interviews in only approximately ten per cent of the cases in the sample. When solicitors are present in interviews they rarely contribute to the proceedings. Neither do social workers. It appears that appropriate adults, including parents, do not normally offer advice to juveniles during questioning or take any steps to ensure that interviews are conducted fairly.

Evans and Ferguson (1991) also suggests that when juveniles do not readily admit during questioning the police use a variety of ploys aimed at obtaining a admission. These include the use leading or legal closure questions. On some occasions there is evidence of 'oppressive' questioning. On others, evidence that suspects are persuaded during an interview that they have committed an offence even when the legal components for the offence have not been established or the suspects do not understand the significance of what they are admitting. The use of these ploys is consistent with the findings of McConville et al (1991) in respect of interviews with adult suspects.

Evans and Ferguson (1991) conclude from their examination of interviews with juveniles that there is some support for the idea that they play a crucial part in the 'social construction' of cases. Indeed McConville et al (1991) suggest that the police interview is the principal forum for case construction. The concept of 'case construction' rests on the observation that any police case involves selecting certain 'facts' from the universe of those available. This selection takes place in the context of a complex set of social relationships and negotiations between the public, suspects and the police.

When examining the role of police interviews in the case construction process McConville et al (1991) argue that the rhetoric of the law suggests that the purpose of interviews is to elicit 'facts' from suspects. Interviews, however, have to be understood not only in terms of the skill of the police in uncovering the facts but also in terms of negotiations about what the facts are. An important factor in interviews is that the police are in a position of power in these negotiations. An important context is that, within an adversarial system of justice, the role of the police is to construct the best case for the prosecution. McConville et al (1991) suggest that unreliable confessions are a predictable outcome of routine police practices since the police rarely rely on simple information seeking forms of questioning.

Researchers have drawn attention to those forms of questioning used in police interviews that might lead to unreliable confessions and particularly to the use of leading questions (Lipton 1977, Powers et al 1979, Cahill and Mingay 1986). McConville et al (1991) identify three further types of questions which '*overtly manipulate*' the suspect's decision making. Statement questions confront suspects with 'facts' which they are invited to confirm or deny. They give as an example 'You took the money after displaying a knife and went out and threatened the victim didn't you?'. Legal closure questions are phrased in legally significant terms in the hope that the suspect will adopt these terms in their answer. Imperfect syllogistic questions attempt to persuade suspects to accept the truth of a disputable or erroneous proposition by asking them to accept that it follows from the acceptance of other statements which have already been agreed.

It has already been suggested that some juveniles may be psychologically vulnerable in police interviews both by reason of their age and because of their reaction to the experience of arrest and detention. This issue of has been explored by Godjonsson and Clark (1986) and Gudjonsson and MacKeith (1988) who have identified two categories of erroneous confession evidence associated with psychological vulnerability. Coerced – compliant confessions occur when suspects confess for some immediate instrumental gain, for example, to gain release from custody. Coerced – internalised confessions occur when suspects are persuaded during the interview process that they have committed a crime and accept suggestions made to them by the police. McConville et al (1991) report that their research indicates a third category which is the coerced-passive confession. Here suspects adopt words which amount to a confession without understanding that they have even made an admission.

Whilst the Evans and Ferguson (1991) research provides some support for the observations of McConville et al (1991) and Godjonsson and Clark (1986) one limitation of their analysis is that it is largely qualitative. It rests on case examples thought to be illustrative of the routine processes that characterise police interviews. In this respect their approach is similar to the methodology adopted by McConville et al (1991). As a consequence both Evans and Ferguson (1991) and McConville et al (1991) make no attempt to provide a precise quantitative analysis of interview material. One of the main purposes of the present study is to make a greater attempt at quantification by measuring, for example, the frequency of occurrence of the use of particular types of question and of the use of persuasive tactics.

The research aims

The aims of the present research study are:

First, to use the Evans and Ferguson (1991) data to explore the factors associated with admissions or denials as outcomes of police interviews with juveniles. In this analysis an admission refers to those cases where the police record of the interview states that the juvenile has made a full confession to all the elements of the alleged offence. Any cases where the police record was not clear on this point, for example cases where suspects made damaging admissions that fell short of a full confession, were eliminated from the analysis. Previous research (Leiken 1970, Softley et al 1980, Baldwin and McConville 1980, Irving and McKenzie 1989, Moston et al 1992) suggests that factors affecting whether suspects admit or deny offences during police interviews include, for example, the suspects sex and age, the strength of the evidence against them, their criminal history or the type and seriousness of the offence they are accused of.

Second, to provide a more comprehensive qualitative and quantitative analysis of the conduct of interviews with juvenile suspects in the Evans and Ferguson (1991) case sample. This is based on a sample of taped interviews relating to those cases where the police record states that the juvenile has made a full confession or where the record contains no clear statement about the outcome of the interview. The analysis is concerned to:

    i.   examine some basic features of juvenile interviews including the time of day that they take place, their duration, the number of officers present, the numbers and types of appropriate adults, and the proportion of interviews that are second and subsequent interviews.

   ii. ascertain how frequently and in what circumstances juveniles readily admit to their offences.

  iii. measure the frequency with which the police use persuasive techniques in an attempt to obtain a confession and to see if these are used when juveniles are reluctant to admit to the offences they are accused of.

  iv. identify the types of persuasive tactics that the police use in interviews and the frequency of their use.

   v. measure the frequency of use of leading and legal closure forms of questions.

  vi. examine the role of appropriate adults, social workers and solicitors.

Third, to examine the relationship between the interview content, the outcome of the interview as recorded by the police and the final disposal of the case. The analysis concentrates on those cases where the police record states that the juvenile has admitted the offence or where it is unclear whether they have admitted or denied. If there is any evidence that the police claim that juveniles have admitted offences when they have not then clearly this would be a matter of some concern. This is particularly important for those cases disposed of by means of a caution because, as has already been stated, the evidential basis for decisions in these cases, including confession evidence, is not open to public scrutiny. It may also be important for those cases going to court if tapes of interviews are not examined, for example, during the process of case review by the CPS or by defence solicitors

The study focuses on the conduct of police interviews with juveniles, rather than adults, on the assumption that this might be a critical site for examining the routine practices of the police for at least two reasons. If a key concern is with the inappropriate or illegitimate use of manipulative or persuasive techniques then it might be expected that these are least likely to be used with groups that can be considered 'at risk'. Second, it might be expected that they would be reserved for 'serious' offences. Conversely if there is evidence that the police use persuasive techniques with juveniles committing relatively minor offences then this might be indicative of the routine use of these interview practices. They may not just be restricted to 'hard' cases

The research methodology

Factors associated with admission or denials

The Evans and Ferguson (1991) database is used for the analysis of factors associated with admissions or denials. Data for this research was collected over a nine month period commencing in May 1990. The sample was collected from two police stations in each of three sub-divisions within a single police force making a total of six stations in all. One aspect of the research was to examine different types of inter-agency consultation process. Of the three sub-divisions chosen for the study two were served by bureaux and the third by a panel system thought to be typical of that used in all the remaining sub-divisions within the force. Researchers based themselves successively in the six sub-divisional police stations for the period required to collect the sample quota for each area. Random samples were constructed by taking all juveniles arrested or reported for summons for criminal offences during the researchers period at the sub-divisional station. The aim was to collect 100 'cases' in the area covered by the panel and 50 each in those covered by the two bureau. We defined a 'case' in the same sense as the police i.e. each 'case' relating to an incident possibly involving a number of suspects. Thus our 202 'cases' involved 367 individuals. The data collected for each individual included an interview with the arresting and/or interviewing officer, the custody officer and the juvenile liaison officer in the panel system and an analysis of the crime file and observations of those cases that were referred for discussion to the panel or bureau.

The methodology used for the analysis of factors associated with admissions or denials is discussed in detail in Chapter 2. Potentially relevant factors are identified on the basis of previous research and a statistical analysis of the effect of various factors on admissions or denials is conducted using Hiloglinear analysis. There are a number of limitations to this analysis which are discussed in more detail in Chapter 2. One limitation is that it is impossible to know from the Evans and Ferguson (1991) data whether the police use persuasive tactics in interviews and, if they do, in which cases these are used. The present study only provides this information for those cases where the police record of the interview states that they have made a full confession or where the record contains no clear statement about the outcome of the interview. It is not therefore possible to include the use or non-use of persuasive tactics as a factor in the analysis of what determines the outcomes of all the interviews in the Evans and Ferguson (1991) sample. In retrospect it might have been better to have obtained copies of taped interviews for as many of the original Evans and Ferguson (1991) sample of 367 juveniles as are available rather than concentrate on those cases where the police record states that the juvenile has admitted to the offence or when there was no clear outcome recorded. This would have enabled the inclusion of a factor concerned with the use of persuasive techniques in the statistical analysis. A decision was taken, however, when designing the research that it would not be possible to provide an analysis of such a large sample of tapes in the time available.

A second limitation of the factor analysis is that the outcomes of interviews are those recorded by the police on the crime file. It cannot be taken for granted that case summaries accurately reflect the interview content in all cases (Baldwin and Bedward 1991).

The analysis of taped interviews

Of the sample of 367 juveniles used as the basis for the Evans and Ferguson (1991) research it was estimated that there were 273 whose interviews at the police station were tape recorded. At the time of the research it was not force policy to tape record all interviews. According to the police record of interview 186 of this group (68 per cent) either admitted the offence or it was not clear whether they had admitted or not. The police were asked to supply copies of tapes for these 186 interviews. This resulted in 164 copies of taped interviews which is 88.2 per cent of the number requested. Most of this discrepancy is accounted for by the fact that some of the interviews were not taped as originally thought. The interviews took place during a nine month period from May 1990.

These tapes were transcribed and inserted into the Evans and Ferguson (1991) research database. This enabled the interview to be considered in relation to our knowledge of the case as a whole from the point of arrest to a final decision about disposal. Again the precise methodology used to analyse the sample of taped interviews is discussed in Chapter 3. This consists of a quantitative analysis using a coding framework and qualitative analysis using case examples to illustrate commonly observed features and processes. The limitations of this methodology are discussed in detail in Chapter 3. One limitation is that the sample of taped interviews is relatively small. This particularly affects the quantitative analysis of the relationship between interview content, the outcome as recorded in the case summary and the final disposal of the case, as relatively small number are involved.

A general limitation of this study is that the data is drawn from one police force at one point in time. Since the period when the interviews, which the object of this study, were conducted the force in question claims to have made considerable changes to it interviewing practices. These include more rigourous supervision of cases and more focussed distance learning training schemes. In addition it is impossible to say to what extent the interview techniques used in this force are representative of those used in other forces although there is no particular reason to think that they are not.

FACTORS ASSOCIATED WITH
ADMISSIONS OR DENIALS

This Chapter is concerned with the factors associated with admissions or denials made during police interviews with juveniles. It builds on previous research that has identified a number of variables that appear to be associated with the outcomes of interviews (Leiken 1970, Neubauer 1974, Baldwin and McConville 1980, Softley et al 1980, Mitchell 1983, Irving and McKenzie 1989, Moston et al 1992). These include the age of suspects, their criminal histories, the seriousness and type of offences which they commit and the strength of the evidence against them. It is intended to place the interview process, which is discussed in the following Chapter, in a broader context. It also serves as a corrective to the view that the sole or most important determinant of the outcome of interviews is police interview techniques.

Irving and Hilgendorf (1980) discuss police interviews in terms of the chain of decisions that have to be made by both suspects and interviewers. The suspect must decide to speak or to remain silent; to tell the truth, to be evasive or to lie. These decisions in turn may be affected by a number of factors such as previous experience of police interviews, knowledge of the police evidence, advice received from solicitors or the likely consequences of confessing. The interviewer must decide how much evidence there is that the suspect is guilty and whether the primary purpose of the interview is to eliminate the suspect from the enquiry or to obtain further information or a confession. This in turn may affect the interview strategy adopted.

Moston et al (1992) adopt a more structured approach to the interview as a decision making process. Their 'interaction process' model is concerned with the relationships between three sets of variables and the relevance of these to understanding police interviews. The first set of variables consists of the background characteristics of the case and the suspect which as previous research has indicated, might render the suspect more or less likely to confess. These characteristics include such factors as the age, sex, offence type and severity and the criminal history of the suspect. The second set of variables are contextual factors that might have a bearing on the behaviour of the interviewer and the suspect. The main contextual factors are legal advice and the strength of the evidence although others such as the location of the police station, the number of interviews or the time spent in custody might come into play. Strength of evidence is likely to be a key contextual factor as this can affect both the interviewers and the suspects' behaviour. When the evidence is weak the range of techniques available to the interviewer is limited but when it is strong the interviewer may manipulate the suspect's decision by using the evidence as a persuasive technique to obtain a confession. Similarly the suspect's decision about whether to confess or deny is likely to be affected by his or her judgement of the strength of the evidence which the interviewer has access to. There is little point for example in denying an offence when you have been caught red-handed. The third set of variables consists of the interviewer's techniques which themselves may depend on the background and contextual characteristics of the case.

Moston et al (1992) argue that one of the main problems with existing research is that it fails to provide any analysis of the inter relationship between the factors determining the outcome of interviews. It is possible that two separate factors appear to affect the outcome but that when they are combined, the strength and direction of the relationships, neutralise each other so having no discernible effect. Recent years have seen the development of a statistical technique called hiloglinear analysis (Gilbert 1981). This is useful for uncovering the potentially complex relationships among variables in multi-way cross tabulations. It enables the determination, for example, of whether happily married couples are happy because they are married or because they are also rich and healthy (SPSS 1990). This technique is used by Moston et al (1992) and is the one adopted in this analysis.

One limitation of this type of statistical analysis is that the interpretation of the data becomes more difficult as the number of categories in each factor increases. This results in complex multi-way cross tabulation tables with large numbers of cells. In addition if cells contain small numbers then the analysis gives more apparent statistical significance than is justified by the data. In order to avoid this danger only the most parsimonious models should be fitted. This may result in rather crude and simplistic codings for some of the factors included in the analysis.

Previous research

Confessions may be more likely when the evidence is strong (Softley et al 1980, Irving and McKenzie 1989, Moston et al 1992). For example Softley et al (1980) found that those suspects that were detained at the scene of burglaries or observed shop-lifting were more likely to confess. Moston et al (1992) report that 66.7 per cent of the cases where police estimates of the strength of evidence was strong resulted in an admission whereas the admission rate was only 9.9 per cent when the police judged that the evidence was weak.

Some studies find that confession rates vary with age with older suspects being less likely to confess (Leiken 1970, Baldwin and McConville 1980 and Softley et al 1980). Softley et al (1980) is one of two studies that separate out confession rates for juveniles and adults. They found that almost eighty per cent of juveniles made a confession or admission. Whilst Moston et al (1992) found that there was no main affect of age groups on the outcome of interviews, juveniles tended to deny an allegation more frequently than older suspects when there was strong evidence. With moderate evidence juveniles tended to deny less frequently than adults. They interpreted this as evidence for juveniles using inappropriate 'escape' strategies. They are inappropriate because when there is strong evidence denial does not realistically affect the chances of escaping punishment. Leng et al (1989) found that 60.7 per cent of juveniles made a full confession, 20.0 per cent made an incriminating statement, 17.9 per cent denied the offence and 1.5 per cent refused to answer any questions with one juvenile too drunk to remember the incident.

The results of research which has explored the relationship between the suspect's criminal histories and the outcomes of interviews is more confusing. Neubauer (1974) and Softley et al (1980) found that suspects without criminal records are more likely to confess than those with. Baldwin and McConville's (1980) results suggest that the relationship goes in the opposite direction. In their sample those with criminal records were slightly more likely to confess than those without. Moston et al (1992) suggest that there is a more complex relationship between these two factors. Admissions rose steadily with strength of evidence but the rate at which they rose differed according to whether or not the suspect has a criminal history. When there was strong evidence those with a criminal record were less likely to confess and more likely to exercise their right to silence than those without. When suspects had a criminal record and legal advice they were less likely to admit than those with legal advice but without a criminal record.

The evidence on the relationship between the type of offence and the outcome of interviews is also somewhat contradictory. Mitchell (1983) and Neubauer (1974) found that those accused of property offences confessed more frequently than those accused of crimes against the person. Moston et al (1992) suggest that the explanation of this finding is that the police are more likely to have physical evidence such as stolen goods or finger prints for property offences than for offences against the person. This question of the kind and strength of evidence in relation to different types of offences is particularly pertinent to juveniles. Evans and Ferguson (1991) found that the majority of crimes against the person in their sample of juveniles involved fights between peers, who knew each other, and where there was a history of disputes. The contribution of suspects and victims was often difficult to untangle. The one arrested was often the one left standing up! In the absence of any independent witnesses the only evidence in these cases was the complainant's statement together with any evidence of injury. Moston et al (1992) found that there was no relationship between offence category and the outcome of interviews, either on its own or in interaction with the strength of evidence, for a sample including adults and juveniles.

Factors associated with admissions or denials

There are nine variables that are available from the Evans and Ferguson (1991) data and which on the basis of previous research, are potentially relevant to the outcome of interviews. These are:

1. *Sex of suspect*

2. *Age of suspect*. This was grouped into 0–13; 14; 15; and 16 which produced four groups of roughly equal size.

3. *Police Sub-Division*. Evans and Ferguson (1991) describe how police perceptions of the areas that they worked in differed markedly. Two critical differences were the type of housing and the seriousness and volume of crime. The spectrum of residential areas ranged from '*a posh, up market, dormitory for commuting managers*' to '*one of the most notorious council housing estates in Europe – a breeding ground for crime*'. Similarly police perceptions of the volume of work in different police stations ranged from '*relatively peaceful*' to '*one of the busiest stations in the force*'. The ethos of the stations, which appeared to permeate their working practices, including their approaches to interrogation, tended to reflect the nature of the areas in which they were located.

4. *Criminal history* Those with or without previous convictions.

5. *The arresting officers judgement of the seriousness of the offence.* This may affect the determination with which interviewers attempt to obtain a confession, particularly in those cases where there is strong evidence linking the suspect to the offence. Arresting officers interviewed for the Evans and Ferguson (1991) research were asked whether or not they considered the offence 'serious'. Responses were dichotomised into 'serious' and 'non-serious' offences.

6. *The strength of the evidence.* This was coded into strong, medium and weak. An attempt was made to arrive at consistent judgements of the strength of evidence by employing criteria culled from the cases in the

sample as a whole. For examples evidence was coded 'strong' when suspects were caught red handed by the police, were detained by store detectives having been observed shop-lifting or identified by witnesses to the crime who knew the suspect. It was coded medium when a suspect fitting a witness description was apprehended at or near the scene of the crime or was in possession of stolen goods. It was coded weak when there was no evidence or the only evidence was an incriminating statement from a co-defendant or the word of the complainant against the suspect as in the case of many juvenile assaults.

There are a number of reasons why measuring the strength of evidence is inherently problematic. In practice interviews tend to take place at an early stage in the investigative process when all the evidence relevant to a final decision on the case may not have been gathered. The evidence, and evaluations of the evidence, may change as the case progresses through the decision making process up to and including court. In addition, as recent cases of miscarriages of justice demonstrate, what is regarded as irrefutable evidence at one point in time may be discredited at another.

7. *Offence type.* Categorised into offences against property and offences against the person. The majority of offences against the person in our case sample consist of physical or sexual assaults but any offences that included an element of violence or the threat of violence, for example robbery, were included in this category.

8. *The seriousness of the offence.* The concept of seriousness has been relatively neglected in criminological analysis although Rossi et al (1974) suggest that the seriousness of criminal acts *'represents a conceptual dimension of criminality indispensable in everyday discourse, in legal theory and practice, and in sociological work'*. This begs the question of how seriousness should be judged.

There has been a considerable amount of research on the question of whether there is any social consensus about judgements of offence seriousness (Sellin and Wolfgang 1964, Rose 1966, Walker 1971, Durant et al 1972, Hood 1972, Rossi et al 1974, Pease et al 1976, Sparks 1977, Walker 1978, Pease 1988). Fitzmaurice and Pease (1986) drawn two main conclusions from their review of this research. First individuals can make confident judgements of the seriousness of offences even though they are unable to be specific about how they arrive at these judgements. Second there is a remarkable degree of consensus on judgments of offence seriousness across time, between cultures and among social groups. This is sufficient to encourage the recognition of 'seriousness' as a dimension of legal decision making that is basic and comprehensible.

One problem with using the official labels attached to offences when measuring their seriousness is that these may *'fail to get behind these labels to where true seriousness is said to lie'* (Parker et al 1989). For example Evans and Ferguson (1991) suggest that the organised and systematic burglary of houses in order to steal electrical equipment worth thousands of pounds and the opportunistic theft of an empty tool box from an open garage may both be charged and recorded as burglary of a dwelling.

In order to try to measure the 'true' seriousness of offences Evans and Ferguson (1991) use arresting officers descriptions of the incident leading to the arrest. These vignettes of the circumstances and nature of the offence include the money value of any loss or damage and the degree of any injuries sustained by victims. Independent rankers were invited to rank the offences of all the individuals in the case sample. As expected from the results of previous research the level of statistical agreement between rankers is extremely high. The rank order is then used to assign a seriousness of offence score to each individual in the sample with 1 being the most serious offence and 367 the least. For the purposes of this analysis these are collapsed into three groups of high medium and low scores

9. *Legal or social work advice.* Unlike Moston et al (1992) the Evans and Ferguson (1991) data does not allow us to know in each case whether a solicitor or social worker had been consulted prior to the interview. This variable identifies only those cases where a solicitor or social worker is present in the interview.

Outcomes are categorised into admissions or denials. The original Evans and Ferguson (1991) data has a third category of 'unclear' where the police record of the interview gave no clear indication of whether there was an admission or denial. Admissions that fall short of a full confession are included in this category. It was decided to remove cases in the unclear category (65 of the 356 cases for which this information is available) as this unnecessarily complicates the analysis and the focus of interest is on factors associated with admissions or denials.

Some sample characteristics

The distribution of the sample by age and sex is shown in Table 2.1. Girls comprised 13.9 per cent of the total sample which is similar to the proportions found in other studies (Morris and Giller 1987). There was only one ten year old suspect and the proportion of eleven and twelve year olds was relatively small being 6.7 per cent and 5.6 per cent respectively. The two largest age groups are fifteen and sixteen year olds.

Table 2.1 Number of suspects by sex and age groups.

	Age Group	Male	Female	Totals
	10–13	70	12	82
	14	62	11	73
	15	77	19	96
	16	100	8	108
Totals		309	50	359

Missing values=8.

The distribution of 'offences' in our case sample is shown in Table 2.2. The offences committed by this sample of juveniles cover a wide range from threats to kill to minor motoring offences. As with official Criminal Statistics the majority are property offences. Evans and Ferguson (1991) report that the proportion of girls in the sample is relatively small so that it is difficult to make any inferences about differences in offence patterns relative to boys. One readily apparent difference in offending patterns are that girls are less likely to be charged with robbery, burglary or taking cars without the owners consent and more likely to be charged with shop-lifting and other types of theft.

Table 2.2 Numbers and types of primary offences

Property Offences	No	Violence Offences	No
Arson	6	Threats to kill	1
Burglary dwelling	24	Robbery	19
Burglary other	44	Grievous bodily harm	1
Theft from a shop	56	Actual bodily harm	31
Other theft/handling	52	Indecent assault	3
Theft from a person	3	Offensive weapon	4
Criminal damage	52	Public order	8
TWOC	24		
Allowing to be carried	3		
Driving whilst disq. by age	4		
Trespass (enclosed premises)	3		
Possession cannabis	3		
Totals	274		67
No crime	26		

N = 367

The criminological literature has given little attention to the amount of 'trivia' pushed into the juvenile justice system (Parker et al 1981). The term minor offences is preferred here in acknowledgment of the view, expressed by the police amongst others, that these offences may not be trivial to the victims (Evans and Wilkinson 1990). An important context for this study is that the vast majority of the cases in the sample have committed minor offences.

The serious offences committed by individuals in the sample would be considered 'serious' by any standard. For example the offence ranked the most serious by our independent rankers involves the burglary of four dwelling houses and the theft of two cars to the value of £10,000. Those committed by the majority of the sample, however, consist of barely distinguishable and relatively minor offences. When rank seriousness scores are grouped into eight equal groups the most serious offence in the least serious group is the theft of a packet of biscuits worth 75 pence and that in the next group the theft of an alarm clock worth £9.99. Approximately 30 per cent of the individuals in our case sample were dealt with for theft or damage under £10, minor public order offences or no crime at all. A further 25 per cent were dealt with for theft or damage under £25 or minor assaults usually between peers.

Although offences may be objectively minor this is not necessarily the way in which they are seen by the police. Their responses indicate that 55 per cent of all reported incidents, including those in which it transpires that no crime has been committed (7.1 per cent of the sample), are regarded as 'serious' by arresting officers (Evans and Ferguson 1991).

Factors associated with the outcome of interviews

Table 2.3 Factors associated with the outcomes of interviews: Summary of statistical associations.

Factor affecting outcome	Degrees of freedom	Partial Chi-Square	Significance
Sex	1	1.2	n.s.
Age group	3	0.3	n.s.
Police Subdivision	2	10.9	$p<0.05$
Criminal history	1	10.3	$p<0.001$
Arresting Officer's view of Seriousness	1	0.8	n.s.
Evidence	2	36.2	$p<0.001$
Offence type	2	1.5	n.s.
Seriousness	2	6.7	$p<0.05$
Legal/SW advice	1	0.3	n.s.
Evidence x seriousness	4	9.9	$p<0.05$
Criminal History x Subdivision	2	21.3	$p<0.001$
Seriousness x Subdivision	4	9.7	$p<0.05$

The statistical associations between factors potentially determining the outcomes of interviews is shown in Table 2.3. The four main factors affecting outcomes are the strength of evidence, the suspects criminal history, the seriousness of the offence and the police subdivision in which the interview took place. Table 2.3 suggests that sex, age group, offence type, or the presence or absence of legal advice are not main affects on outcomes for this sample. Neither is the arresting officers' judgement of whether or not it is a serious offence.

There are similarities and differences with Moston et al's (1992) findings. For their data they identified three main associations with outcomes. These were the strength of evidence, the interviewers perception of offence severity and legal advice. Curiously they do not explain why they excluded the factor of the police station where the interview took place even though this is statistically associated with outcomes for their data.

There might be a number of reasons why this could be an influence on interview outcomes. For example the police literature suggests that 'cop culture' may vary not only from force to force but from station to station (Holdaway 1983, Reiner 1985). This might affect interview styles because interview training is provided mainly on the job. Interview styles and techniques in turn might affect outcomes.

For Moston et al's (1992) data the age group, criminal history and the offence category were not main factors affecting outcomes although age and criminal histories affected second order interactions. The different findings concerning legal advice is not surprising. Our evidence suggests that only a small proportion of juveniles seek legal advice and, as we shall see, if solicitors or social workers attend interviews they almost never contribute to the proceedings.

That neither study finds that the age group is a main factor affecting outcomes is surprising given previous research findings. Moston et al's (1992) sample contained juveniles and adults. Given that the former are thought to confess significantly more frequently than the latter one would have expected this to be reflected in their results. Similarly this sample contains cases distributed across the whole range of the juvenile age group. It might have been expected that older juveniles would confess less frequently than younger ones. For example they may be more willing and able to assert their rights or more likely to have previous convictions making them less ready to admit.

The four factors having the main effect on outcomes in this study are discussed in turn below.

Strength of evidence

Table 2.4 shows the relationship between the strength of evidence and the outcome of the interviews. The strength of evidence has a marked effect on the rate of admissions. With strong evidence the admission rate reaches 77.9 per cent which is similar to Moston et al's (1992) finding. Table 2.4 also suggests that the admission rate remains relatively high even when the evidence is weak bearing in mind that this category includes some cases where there was no evidence. This suggests that juveniles may be more willing to confess than adults whatever the strength of the evidence.

Table 2.4 Strength of evidence and the outcomes of interviews

Strength of evidence	Outcome of interview		
	No of cases	% of admissions	% of denials
Strong	145	77.9	22.1
Medium	74	51.4	48.6
Weak	72	30.6	69.4

Missing values=76

Criminal history

Table 2.5 shows the relationship between the criminal history of suspects and the outcomes of interviews. Those with previous convictions are less likely to confess than those without. This may be open to a number of interpretations. For example those with previous convictions may have more experience of police interrogation techniques and therefore may be better able to resist them and/or have a greater interest in declaring their innocence. On the other hand they may be more susceptible to arrest and questioning for offences which they have not committed.

Table 2.5 Criminal history and the outcome of interviews

Criminal History	Outcome of interview		
	No of cases	% of admissions	% of denials
No previous Convictions	130	67.7	32.3
Previous Convictions	161	52.8	47.2

Missing values=76

The seriousness of offences

Table 2.6 shows the relationship between the seriousness of offences as judged by independent rankers and the outcomes of interviews. Those committing offences judged the most serious are less likely to admit. Again this might be open to a number of interpretations. For example admissions rates may fall as the stakes in terms of punishment rise. The finding that admission rates in the other two groups are similar is not surprising. This is consistent with the observation that the offences in the sample as a whole consist of a small number of serious offences and a mass of barely distinguishable and relatively minor ones.

Table 2.6 Offence seriousness and the outcomes of interviews

Offence seriousness	Outcome of interview		
	No of cases	% of admissions	% of denials
High	100	50.0	50.0
Medium	93	63.4	36.6
Low	98	65.3	34.7

Missing values=76

Police subdivision

The relationship between the police subdivision in which the interview took place and the outcome of interviews is shown in Table 2.7. This shows that there are significant differences in admission rates depending on the subdivision in which the interview takes place. It was not possible to measure whether outcomes varied with the six individual police stations that were involved in the Evans and Ferguson (1991) research using the hiloglinear analysis. The inclusion of a six value variable has a significant impact of the number of cells in the analysis and leads to the problem of small numbers discussed earlier. A separate analysis of admission rates for individual police stations suggests however, that rates vary with these (Chi-Square = 22.8, d.f. 5, p>.001). This relationship is maintained even when other variables, including strength of evidence, seriousness of offence and criminal histories are controlled for individually. One tentative interpretation could be that interview styles may vary from station to station and have an impact on outcomes. This would be consistent with the thesis that police stations have their own ethos and culture. It would also be consistent with the thesis that police interviewing techniques takes place on the job. If individual police stations develop their own distinctive approaches then the dominance of on-the-job training might ensure that these are passed on to new recruits to the station.

It is not possible to provide any direct evidence in support of these speculations from this study. This hypothesis obviously requires a closer and different kind of examination. It is interesting to note, however, that Moston et al (1992) also found that the police station at which the interview took place is a main effect on outcomes but, for reasons which they do not explain, they did not pursue this in their analysis.

Table 2.7 Police subdivision and the outcome of interviews

Offence seriousness	Outcome of interview		
	No of cases	% of admissions	% of denials
1	86	75.6	24.4
2	61	60.7	39.3
3	144	49.3	50.7

Missing values = 76

Interactions between variables

Evidence x seriousness x outcome

When there is strong evidence admission rates are lower for suspects accused of offences judged the most serious (68.9 per cent) than for those judged the least (85.7 per cent). Similarly when the evidence is moderate there is a steady increase in admission rates with a decrease in the seriousness of the offence. There is no obvious relationship between admission rates and the seriousness of the offence when the evidence is weak the rate being 17.6 per cent for those judged the most serious offences and 15.4 per cent for those judged the least. This result perhaps indicates that when suspects realise they are being accused of a serious offence they are less likely to admit even when the evidence against them is strong. This could simply be a calculation about the consequences of admitting in these circumstances.

Criminal history x subdivision x outcome

There is a marked difference in admission rates for those with and without criminal histories in different subdivisions. In one subdivision rates of admission are similar for those with and without previous convictions at 79.5 per cent and 72.3 per cent respectively. In the other two subdivisions rates of admission for those with previous convictions are 50.0 per cent and 42.5 per cent and for those without 69.7 per cent and 62.0 per cent. One explanation for this might be that suspects in these two subdivisions tended to have a larger number of previous convictions than in the other. There is no relationship between previous convictions, strength of

22

evidence and outcomes. So there is little support here for the thesis that those with previous convictions are more likely to be arrested and interviewed for offences which they did not commit. There is more support for the thesis that those with previous convictions are more likely to deny because the stakes for them in terms of punishment are higher or because they have more experience of interrogations and are therefore better able to resist any pressure to confess.

Seriousness x subdivision x outcome

Admission rates for those offences judged the least serious varied markedly between subdivisions. In one subdivision the rate was 91.0 per cent compared to approximately 50 per cent in the other two. There is no obvious difference between admission rates for offences of high or medium seriousness between the three subdivisions. Admission rates for the most serious offences are consistently lower than those for the moderately serious. One possible explanation for the high admission rates for the least serious offences in one subdivision lies in the nature of a significant proportion of the offences committed here. This subdivision contained a new purpose built shopping centre that is said by the police to attract juveniles from all over the region. This generated a significant number of minor shop-lifting offences. The fact that these offences were minor, and that suspects were most frequently stopped and detained by store detectives or security guards having been observed in the act, may account for an admission rate of 91. per cent.

Discussion

The findings provide some tentative support for the proposition that confession rates for juveniles are higher than those for mixed age samples or samples of adults. Moston et al (1992) estimate, on the basis of a mixed sample of adults and juveniles, that 41.8 per cent admitted that they had committed an offence, 41.6 per cent denied and 16.6 per cent neither admitted or denied. This compares with Softley et al's (1980) estimate that, according to the police record, almost 80 per cent of the juveniles their sample made a full confession or an incriminating admission. This is similar to Leng et al's (1989) finding that 60.7 per cent of juveniles made a full confession and 20.0 per cent an incriminating admission whilst the corresponding figures for adults are 42.2 per cent and 27.7 per cent respectively. The latter study relies on the researchers own judgements of the outcomes of interviews rather than the police record. It is not strictly comparable to the the data from this study which shows that 48.6 per cent (173) of juvenile suspects made a 'full and frank admission' and in 18.3 per cent (65) of the cases there was no clear outcome to the interview according to case summaries contained in the crime files. Differences between rates of denial in this study and Leng's are even more striking.

Leng et al found that 17.5 per cent of the juveniles in their sample denied the offence whereas in the present study the figure was almost twice the rate reported by Leng being 33.1 per cent (118) of the cases.

One possible interpretation of these differences is that they might be the result of using different definitions of confessions and admissions. An alternative interpretation is that any difference in rates is due to differences in sample characteristics as the samples are drawn from different police forces having potentially different crime and offender profiles in their juvenile populations.

Case characteristics are clearly not the only influence on the outcomes of interviews. The literature on police interrogations has given considerable importance to the effect of interviewing tactics and techniques (Softley et al 1980, Irving and Hilgendorf 1980, Irving and McKenzie 1989, McConville et al 1991). Moston et al (1992) comment that police officers would probably like to think that suspects make confessions because of skilled questioning techniques but they found remarkably few cases in which suspects were persuaded to deviate from their initial response to questioning. This finding echoes that of Irving and McKenzie (1989) who conclude that techniques and tactics have little effect on admission rates. The results of the analysis of taped interviews in the present study give support to this point of view. In approximately three quarters of the cases interviews are perfunctory and routine with no apparent need or attempt on the part of the police to use persuasive tactics in order to obtain a confession.

The main conclusion that can be drawn from the statistical analysis contained in this Chapter is that, in terms of Moston et al's (1992) 'interaction process' model, background and contextual factors are important determinants of the outcomes of interviews. For this study the main factors are: the criminal history of the suspect; the seriousness of the offence; the strength of evidence; and the Sub-Division in which the interview takes place. For Moston et al (1992) the main factors affecting confessions are the strength of evidence, the interviewers perception of the severity of the offence and legal advice. In both studies the strongest relationship is between the strength of evidence and the likelihood of a confession. The stronger the evidence the more likely it is that the suspect will confess with the paradoxical result that confessions are most likely when least necessary to the prosecution case. Again in both studies perceptions of the seriousness of the offence determine the outcome of interviews although they use different measures of seriousness. Finally both Moston et al (1992) and this study provide important cumulative evidence that legal rather than non-legal variables are the main determinants of the outcomes of interviews, the most statistically significant being the strength of evidence against the suspect.

THE INTERVIEW PROCESS

The analysis in this Chapter is based on a sample of 164 taped interviews with juveniles. These are interviews conducted with individuals in the original 367 case sample of the Evans and Ferguson (1991) research. The police were asked to supply copies of taped interviews for all those cases where the police record of the interview stated that the suspect had made a full confession or where the outcome of the interview was not clear from the record. They were able to supply 164 of the original 186 interviews requested as discussed in the introduction to this report.

The context of the interview

The study by Evans and Ferguson (1991) suggests that juveniles are arrested as a matter of routine despite the concerns of the 1981 Royal Commission on Criminal Procedure that arrest is a *'coercive power'* that may cause those detained *'alarm and dismay'*. Even when suspects are 'invited' to the police station for interview, custody officers are reluctant to allow interviewing officers to conduct these except under PACE conditions. Where the police want to interview a juvenile in almost all cases this is done following arrest. The reason given is that custody officers do not want to be responsible for 'prisoners' in the charge room area that have not been arrested.

Juveniles are dealt with in the station charge room along with adults. They are usually detained awaiting the arrival of the appropriate adult, solicitor or social worker. Whether juveniles are detained in a special juvenile detention room or in normal cells depends largely on the facilities available at the station or whether they are in the younger or older age range. The usual length of time that juveniles in the sample were detained at the police station was between one and four hours. This is similar to the duration of detention found in previous research (Softley 1980, Barnes and Webster 1981, McConville et al 1991). The potential utility of arrest and detention is readily acknowledged by police officers. Evans and Ferguson (1991) describe how, in the eyes of some arresting officers, the experience of being arrested and detained in the police station may be a potent deterrent to further offending. It is a *'frightener'*, *'It raises the seriousness for the lad'* and *'it acts as a warning'*. The very fact that juveniles are arrested and detained for questioning by the police may render them psychologically vulnerable.

Some basic interview data

Interviews generally took place in the afternoon between mid-day and six o'clock in the evening (46.9 per cent) or between six o'clock in the evening and midnight (35.9 per cent). Only a small proportion took place between midnight and 6 a.m. (5.5 per cent) or in the morning between 6 a.m. and mid-day (11.6 per cent). Interviews tended to be very brief with the majority taking less than fifteen minutes (71.4 per cent). Although the average length of interviews was around 14 minutes the most frequent length was around 7 minutes. There were no examples of suspects being interviewed more than twice and 92.7 per cent of them were interviewed only once. Suspects were interviewed by a mixture of uniformed officers and plain clothes detectives who were either constables or sergeants. In approximately two thirds of the cases (64.6 per cent) two officers were present at the interview and in the remainder (35.4 per cent) an officer acted alone. Parents, or another relative, attended the interview in 79.9 per cent of cases. Both parents attended in only 6.7 per cent of cases. Social workers acted as the appropriate adult in 18.3 per cent of cases. Solicitors attended in 10.9 per cent of cases and in 4.3 per cent of cases both a solicitor and a social worker were present.

Charges

Evans and Ferguson (1991) report that they had some difficulty in identifying the exact legal offence for which some of the juveniles in their sample were dealt with. This is partly because juveniles are rarely formally charged at the police station, immediately after the interview, as is the case with adults. As a consequence charges are open to negotiation and change during the decision making process. The exact charge may be difficult to locate in the case papers, particularly in those cases that are dealt with by means of a caution or informal warning.

Force policy states that instant charging should be reserved for the most serious offences where there is clearly no practical alternative to prosecution. In the Evans and Ferguson (1991) sample this occurred in 8.4 per cent of cases. This is surprisingly high given the relatively small proportion of serious offences in the sample.

The usual procedure for juveniles is that arresting officers prepare a report for a decision to be made by another officer. Occasionally this may be the duty custody officer but more usually cases are referred for decision to the police juvenile liaison officers or to some form of inter-agency consultation such as a juvenile panel or bureau. Evans and Ferguson

(1991) report that offences in their sample are almost inevitably labelled with the most serious charge possible. For example thefts from the person, whatever the degree of actual or threatened violence used, were charged as robbery with only one exception Thefts from a building were nearly always charged as burglary and if possible the label 'burglary dwelling' was attached. A number of such serious charges involved thefts from garages which were remote from houses and already open. On occasions arresting officers were explicit about their reasons for this. In case B2/9/1 four boys took a football from an open school when they had gone to collect one of the boys' younger brother at the end of the school day. When the arresting officer was asked why they were charged with burglary rather than theft from a building he replied '*because it looks better for our statistics*'

As the process of decision making unfolds the nature of the 'case' may change including the legal labels, and therefore the 'charge', attached to the 'offence' under investigation. For example a juvenile interviewed for suspected theft of a car may eventually be dealt with for taking without the owners consent or allowing himself or herself to be carried. That charges are open to change and negotiation was graphically illustrated during Evans and Ferguson's (1991) observations of panel discussions. The panel was discussing the case of three juveniles that were accused of burglary of a school. This is one of the rare instances where the issue of whether they had in fact admitted to the offence as charged was raised. The juvenile liaison officer read from the interview transcript and it became apparent that they denied either intending to take or taking anything from the school so it would be difficult to sustain a burglary charge. During the interview, however, one of the juveniles admitted writing on the school gate with a spray can. At this point the juvenile liaison officer, half jokingly, exclaimed that although they could not be charged with burglary they could be charged with criminal damage.

An analysis of the sample of 164 taped interviews suggests that a major purpose of some interviews appears to be not only to obtain a confession but also to decide what offence the juvenile should be charged with. In 61.5 per cent of the cases for which taped interviews were obtained suspects were informed at the beginning of the interview precisely what offence they were being questioned about. In the remaining 38.5 per cent of cases they were not directly told what they were accused of. In these cases interviews typically start with questions of the type 'Do you know why you've been arrested?', 'Can you tell me about the incident that happened today?' or 'Do you know why you are here?. Examples include '*Right then J can you tell me what happened yesterday just immediately before I stopped you? What were you doing?* or '*Now we can get on with it. First of all you've been arrested, do you understand why? It's all about the school isn't it – this business with the school?'*. The suspect is then left to give an account of what they think they may have done in their own words. At no point in these interviews are they told precisely why they are being interviewed or why they have been arrested. Even when suspects state at the outset of the interview that they do not know why they are being questioned, interviewers typically respond with comments such as '*Well you must have some idea*'.

Another reason why charges may not be specified at the outset of an interview is that the juveniles may have only been invited to help the police with their enquiries. Yet there is only one instance where it is made clear at the beginning of the interview that the juvenile is not under arrest, is not obliged to answer questions and is free to go whenever he or she wishes. And in only 2.5 per cent of interviews was some other purpose, such as to obtain information or to eliminate suspects from the enquiries, the dominant motive for the interview.

Questioning prior to the formal interview

It is implicit in interviews with this type of opening that there must have been some discussion between the suspect and the interviewing or arresting officer prior to the formal interview. Our original sample was drawn from the custody records of those juveniles who were arrested or invited for interview and therefore we had no opportunity to observe what happened on the streets prior to their arrival at the police station. But on occasions arresting officers quite freely told us about discussions they had had with suspects at the scene of the arrest or in the police car traveling to the station. It is apparent that some of this material is fed into the formal interview process. Indeed some officers were explicit about this: '*I like to have a little chat to get things straight before I switch on the tape*' (Evans and Ferguson 1991). How else could juvenile suspects know what offence the interviewing officer is referring to particularly when they might have been involved in several incidents that might be potential offences?

In some instance there was irrefutable evidence of prior discussion or questioning.

> *C/25/1. The suspect is accused of attempting to steal a television. Early on in the interview the following exchange takes place. There is no mention of a television prior to this point in the interview.*
>
> *PC. Did you actually go into the toilet?*
>
> *Sus. No.*
>
> *PC. You didn't go into the toilet?*
>
> *Sus. I didn't even go past the first office that you said the tele was in.*
>
> *PC. I never said the tele was in anywhere.*

Sus. You did.

PC. OK. If I did then that's fair enough. So the TV then that's in question, we are saying and we both agree, is in the office on the right.

Prior questioning is not only carried out by police officers. There are examples of parents, social workers and neighbours questioning suspects and providing information, including information that the suspect has admitted the offence, to the police when making a complaint or reporting the offence. For example, in case C3/221, according to the arresting officer, the juveniles father brought him to the police station after finding cigarettes and a watch hidden under a garden shed. He had questioned his son who had admitted that the knew that the cigarettes were stolen. The arresting officer stated that he also admitted this to him prior to the interview and this is referred to during it.

It is difficult to see how this can be avoided particularly since the point at which investigation turns into accusation is not always clear. On the other hand juveniles appear to be all too willing, encouraged partly by the informality of situations, to make damaging admissions without necessarily realising the implications for themselves. This may be an compelling argument for being particularly meticulous about cautioning, at the first possible opportunity, that what they say may be used as evidence against them.

Ready confessions

In 76.8 per cent (126) of cases suspects readily confessed. This may simply be a consequence of the fact that they have been caught and and are willing to own up to their offending. Indeed this open admission usually occurred in the first sentence or so of the interview and the distinction between those interviews in which the suspects readily admitted and those that they did not was quite clear cut. For example in case A/3/1 the interviewing officer asked immediately after the initial formalities '*Can you tell me in you're own words why you think you are here*' to which the suspect replied '*because I've done a burglary – a break in*'

Moston et al (1992) report a similar finding for their sample of interviews. Admissions tended to be spontaneous and occurred at an early stage of questioning. On some occasions this was in response to the first question even when it was not obviously accusatory for example a general question about the suspect's movements.

Case A2/15/2. The officer asks the juvenile 'Do you want to explain what happened today – the circumstances under which you were arrested?'

Sus. Yes, We were mucking about and I suggested, just as children do (sic), oh let's go shop-lifting. And we were laughing and joking and S said yeh. Well I didn't take him seriously.

29

PC. OK so what time did you go to the shopping centre?

Sus. It was roughly twenty to two.

PC. And what did you do then?

Sus. We walked into the store and proceeded to take items without paying.

The juvenile goes on to describe how he took the goods from the store, how this was the first time he 'had done anything like this' and how at first he did not want to get involved.

C3/43/1. The suspect is told that he has been arrested for burglary. The interviewing officer establishes the components of the offence in the first few sentences by starting with the question:

PC. Can you remember how you got into the house?

Sus. I climbed through the bedroom window.

PC. Do you remember how you got out of the house?

Sus. The downstairs window.

P.C. Is that the front or the back ?

Sus. Front.

PC. Do you remember what you took from that house?

Sus. I took a Panasonic video recorder.

In the majority of cases in the sample interviews were perfunctory and routine. This is consistent with the fact that they frequently take a very short time to complete. Indeed it was often hard to understand why some interviews go on as long as they do given that the real business is often over in the first few minutes.

Having established that the suspect is willing to admit early on in the interview two other issues are commonly addressed. The first is whether there is anything else that the suspect would like '*to get off your chest – after all you don't want us coming around again do you?*' In 11.0 per cent (18) of the cases there was detailed questioning about offences, other than the main subject of the interview, that might be taken into account in clearing up crimes. Second, it would appear that, particularly if the interviewing officer intends to recommend a caution or an informal warning, it helps if they can record on the crime file that the juvenile says they are sorry for what they have done. Again this is often routinised in the interview process.

Case A2/4/1. The incident that led to the arrest involved an alleged assault. The suspect's brother had caused some damage to a shop window. When the shop owner came out to investigate he was confronted with a group of lads. The suspect's account in the interview was that he got into a scuffle with the shop owner after the latter had threatened his brother. He admitted that he had hit the shop owner but claimed that this was in the cause of defending his brother. At the end of the interview the interviewing officer asks

PC. Don't you wish to add something?

Sus. What?

PC. I thought you might have done

Sus. What?

PC. I can't tell you what to say

Sus. No

PC. Is there something you want to say?

Sus. I don't know

PC. Don't you know what to say, for what you've done?

Sus. Sorry

PC. That's it. Thank you. This is the notice I told you about at the start of the interview.....

In 8.5 per cent (14) of the cases in the sample the suspects readily confessed even when there was no other evidence against them or the evidence was weak. One possibility is that they confessed because they had committed the offence. But this does raise the issue of the reliability of uncorroborated confession evidence and the possibility that some juveniles may confess simply to ensure that they are released from an uncomfortable and threatening situation.

Police interview techniques and tactics

Thirty eight (23.2 per cent) of the suspects in the case sample did not readily confess in the early stages of the interview. There is a strong relationship between the readiness with which juveniles confess and the use of persuasive tactics with the latter more likely to be used when suspects do not readily confess (Chi-Square=60.6 DF=1 p=.001). There is a statistically significant relationship between the seriousness of the offence and the use of persuasive tactics (Chi-Square=6.045 d.f.=2 p=.0487). Persuasive tactics are more likely to be employed for serious offences.

This latter finding corresponds with that of Irving and McKenzie (1989) who note that, for the purposes of defining interrogation strategies, the cases in their sample fell into three general categories. Trivial cases in which the evidence prior to interrogation is sufficient to charge, serious cases in which the evidence is overwhelming and the suspect is aware of the evidence, and serious cases in which either the evidence is weak or in which there are either issues of intention or legal definition to wrestle with. They suggest that tactics are rarely used in the first two categories of cases but are mainly reserved for the third.

The analysis of taped interviews suggests that various types of tactics are used by the police in interviews with juveniles. The fact that juveniles tend to offend in groups and to implicate each other in interviews (which they did in 52.4 per cent (86) of the cases in the sample) enables the police to play suspects off against each other in order to try to achieve confessions. Apart from pointing out contradictions between the statements of different suspects or witnesses tactics also include pointing out contradictions within the suspects' own account. Suspects are confronted directly with the evidence for example if they had been found in possession of stolen goods. Another tactic consists of variations on the themes of 'there is no point in denying involvement in the offence because the truth will come out' and/or 'you'll feel better for getting it of your chest'. It is often used in combination with other tactics such as pointing out contradictions between the suspects account and those of other suspects, telling the suspect that this is a way of avoiding the police coming around to arrest and interview him or her again or hinting that the police have definite evidence linking the suspect to the offence. These tactics may be used singly or in combination in individual interviews and the proportionate use of them is shown in Table 3.1.

Table 3.1 The proportionate use of tactics in interviews with juveniles

	Number of Interviews	%
Interviewer points out contradiction between suspects' and co-defendants' account	21	19.1
Interviewer points out contradiction between suspects' and witnesses account	18	16.4
Interviewer points out contradiction in suspect's own account	15	13.6
Suspect confronted with evidence other than that of co-defendant or witness statement	30	27.3
The truth will come out/you'll feel better for getting it off your chest	26	23.6
Total	110	100

A useful point of comparison is the findings of Softley et al (1980) who identified the use of at least one tactic in 60 per cent of initial interviews. The most common tactic, cited in 22 per cent of interviews, was to point out contradictions in the suspect's account or between suspects'accounts and those of other witnesses. In 13 per cent of the interviews the police stressed the overwhelming evidence against the suspect and this was presented in such a way as to make a denial seem pointless. In 15 per cent of the interviews the police seemed to hint or bluff that other evidence might be forthcoming and used this to suggest to the suspect that the truth would inevitably emerge. In 7 per cent of interviews more coercive tactics were used including the threat of further detention.

Scientific evidence linking the the suspect to the crime was rarely introduced directly in the interviews included in this sample of taped interviews. There are however examples of interviewers stating or hinting that this type of evidence, for example finger print evidence, would be or had been found and that therefore there was no point in denying the offence.

> *Case C2/50/1. In this case the suspect is being questioned about a series of burglaries. He has admitted to one but the interviewing officers are using a range of tactics, including the Mr Nice and Mr Nasty routine, to persuade him to admit to others. The first interview concludes with the suspect being sent back to the cells for 'some thinking time'. This exchange takes place in the second interview.*
>
> *PC2. It's your MO isn't it, your style. They're all your style round there.*
>
> *Sus. Um*
>
> *PC2. You admit that?*
>
> *Sus. Yeh*
>
> *PC1. It's time to rub the slate clean and start again. Start again, that's a figure of speech that is. Start afresh.*
>
> *Sus. Don't know nothing about it.*
>
> *PC2. So if we've got any fingerprints from the jobs then and your fingerprints turn up, we've got your name.*
>
> *Sus. You what?*
>
> *PC2. Fingerprints turned up at the jobs. Right. We've got your name and we can put your name forward which cuts down a lot of sifting through files.*
>
> *Sus. Yeh, but they won't.*
>
> *PC2. Why not?*
>
> *Sus. Cos I didn't do them.*
>
> *PC1. Who did?*
>
> *Sus. I don't know*
>
> *PC2. You're that sure*
>
> *Sus. I'm positive. No finger prints will come up on me*
>
> *PC1. So you're covering for your mates then?*
>
> *Sus. Whether they did it I don't know.*
>
> *PC1. Well the way I look at it is, either you did it or your mates did it.*

As has been suggested one of the most frequently used tactics is to state that the truth is bound to come out eventually and therefore there is no point in denying the offence. In addition suspects may be told that owning up is a way of avoiding the police coming around to arrest and interview them again or interviewers may hint that the police have definite evidence linking the suspect to the offence.

> *Case A1/21/1 In this case the suspect was being interviewed about the theft of a bike from the garage of a private house. His name had been given to the police.*
>
> *PC2. We know you're involved in it and we are not going to let it rest until we find out the truth. So you might as well tell us now so you can get it off your chest. Once it's done it's finished isn't it. It's off your chest then out of the way and your mum can sleep of a night time, you can sleep of a night time properly. Because if you don't get it out now, we're going to come back and we'll find out. We've got to find out because we've got so much here that says it's not right, and if we didn't put it to you it won't look right at the end of the day. We'll be criticised because we haven't done what we should have done. Now I don't blame you for sticking out to what you have done because I would in the same circumstances, but we've got too much on you mate to let it stay as it is. Now you get a knack of talking to people and you can tell that something is not right. Now what do you think about that? Em. Come on now, you're on the borderline of telling us the truth. You know what you're saying is not right. You can always start afresh from this point on. It doesn't matter what you've said in the past, get it straight. I know all your mates say don't say nothing, but they're not sat here with you. They're not sat here with this presented to you. Now get it off your chest and say it properly now. What do you think?*

This case is also typical of many interviews where most of the talking is done by the police. Juvenile suspects frequently respond with no more than a 'yeah', 'suppose so' or 'dunno'. The questions may be more important than the answers to the police depending on the stage in the interview that they occur.

The effectiveness of tactics

The question of whether these tactics are effective in persuading suspects to confess is quite another matter. According to the researcher's judgement of the outcome of the interview, rather than that recorded in the police summary, of the 38 cases where suspects did not immediately confess, 19 eventually confessed, 13 clearly denied the offence and in 6 cases there was no full confession or clear denial. The police therefore obtain a confession in 50 per cent of those cases in the sample where the juvenile initially denies the offence and where the police use persuasive tactics. A contingency table analysis suggests that the effectiveness of tactics is independent of the other main factors affecting admissions or denials including strength of evidence, criminal history, the seriousness of the offence and the sub-division in which the interview takes place. Whilst there are no statistically significant relationships a visual inspection of the contingency tables reveals two patterns of potential interest. First, the effectiveness of tactics in obtaining confessions appears to vary with the police station in which the interview takes place although this has to be treated with some caution because of the small numbers involved. There is no obvious explanation of this. Second, in the nineteen cases in which the suspects eventually confessed the evidence against 12 suspects was strong, against 4 medium and against 3 weak. This suggests that it is only in a very small number of cases that suspects are persuaded to confess when other evidence against them is weak. One important qualification to this statement is that, as has been already discussed, assessing the strength of evidence is inherently problematic.

The findings on the use of persuasive tactics have to be placed in the context that in 71.0 per cent (116) of the interviews no discernible tactics are used because suspects readily confess. Together these findings provide some support for the view that interviewing techniques and tactics have a limited overall effect on admission rates compared with the factors identified in Chapter 2.

The final disposals of the 38 cases where juveniles did not readily confess during police interviews are also worth noting. Of the 19 juveniles who eventually made a full confession, 9 were prosecuted, 6 cautioned, 3 informally warned and no further action was taken in the remaining case. Of the 13 juveniles who clearly denied the offence 3 were prosecuted, 4 were cautioned, 2 were informally warned and 4 cases resulted in no further action. Of the 6 cases where there was no full confession or clear denial 4 were prosecuted and 2 were cautioned. There is worrying evidence here that juveniles are cautioned or informally warned even when they have not made a full confession. This is explored further at a later point in the analysis.

The form of police questioning

Apart from examining the use of persuasive techniques researchers have more recently been concerned with the association between the form of police questioning and the reliability of confessions (Gudjonsson and Clarke 1986, McConville et al 1991, McConville et al 1992). The concern is that the answers given by suspects may be influenced by their unwitting acceptance of messages contained in police questions and that this may render their confessions unreliable. McConville et al (1991) identify a number of types of such questions including leading questions, legal closure questions and statements posing as questions. In their more recent study for this Royal Commission McConville and Hodgson et al (1992) elaborate their typology of questions to include questions designed to establish a relationship with the suspect, questions seeking an explanation for apparently incriminating evidence and questions which seek to force the suspect to adopt a police opinion. The latter include statements such as 'Obviously the property is stolen and is passed on: you are not innocent, you know what goes on'. McConville and Hodgson et al (1992) suggest that whilst many of these types of questions may be unproblematical *some are associated with unreliable or wrongful confessions*. These include leading questions, statement questions, legal-closure questions, accusatory questions and those which seek the adoption of a police opinion.

In 74.4 per cent (122) of cases interviewers relied almost exclusively on simple information-seeking questions. This is perhaps unsurprising given that approximately three quarters of the juveniles in the taped interview sample confessed in the first few sentences of the interview and that these interviews tended to be perfunctory and routine. This challenges McConville et al's (1991) assertion that the police interrogations 'only *rarely*' rely on this type of question.

The two main types of 'problematic' questions, used by police interviewers in the sample of taped interviews, are leading and legal closure questions. Leading questions are any question which supplies it's own answer. For example 'so you knew the goods were stolen didn't you'. Legal closure questions are a special type of leading question which seeks to ensure that the suspect provides verbal proof of one element of an offence in a single answer. Leading questions were employed in 19.5 per cent (32) of the cases in the sample and legal closure questions in 12.2 per cent (20) of the cases. Whilst these statistics might be indicative of attempts to exploit the suspects' interrogative suggestibility they cannot tell the whole story. This can only be understood in the context of the interview process as a whole. In some of the interviews there was clear evidence that, although suspects had initially denied being involved in any offence, they later accepted that they were by virtue of the interviewing officers persuasive logic. For example one interviewer suggested to a suspect that they had gone into a school with the intention of stealing something which the suspect strenuously denied. The interviewer then suggested to the boy that he knew that it was wrong to go into the school, that he might *have thought of nicking something* and that that would amount to burglary. In fact the purpose of the interview was to try to obtain information about which of the co-defendants, if any, had started a fire in the school and whether this had been done intentionally. The purpose of persuading the boy that he had done something wrong, and that this could be legally defined as an offence, appeared to be to put pressure on him to tell the truth about the alleged arson.

Interviewers use the 'legal closure' form of question in order to by-pass the necessity of having to establish that the legal components of offences, for example 'recklessness' or the 'intention to permanently deprive', are present. For example in Case A1/14/2 a group of boys had taken a set of goal posts from the school and set them up on a piece of open ground at the rear of a church. As far as the boys were concerned they had established with a teacher that the goal posts were not used and so had 'borrowed' them in order to play football. One of the group had helped the others carry the posts and denied knowing they were stolen.

WPC. So, if they were property to the school, why did you take them? Why did you take them, then?

Sus. To play with them.

WPC. Do you know the difference between right and wrong?

Sus. Yes.

WPC. And is it right or wrong to take property that belongs to somebody else?

Sus. Wrong.

WPC. So, you took property belonging to somebody else which amounts to stealing, that's right, isn't it?

Sus. Yes.

WPC. What part did P have to play in this?

Sus. He just helped us carry them.

WPC. And where did you see him ?

Sus. On the road as we was coming out of the gates.

WPC. And did you tell him where you'd got the posts from?

Sus. Yes.

WPC. So, what, you said you'd taken them from the Brandford School?

Sus. Yes.

WPC. So he knew that they were stolen?

Sus. Yes.

Later the interviewer tries to establish that there was the intention to 'permanently deprive' the school of the posts.

WPC. So you had no intention really of taking the stuff back?

Sus. We was going to take it back when we'd finished with them.

WPC. Nothing was ever decided to take them back, though, was it?

The production of evidence about 'intentions' or 'states of mind' is often central to police interviews with juveniles yet in many ways the most

37

difficult type of evidence to establish. For example the offence of criminal damage requires proof of intention or recklessness. The 'fact' of damage is not enough. It may have been caused accidentally and juveniles often claim that it has been. The legal-closure question short cuts these difficulties.

> *C2/47/3. In this case a girl is being interviewed in connection with fruit that had been stolen from outside a shop. She claimed that she had not participated in the theft directly although she knew what her friends were doing. She had been sitting on a wall around the corner.*
>
> *Sus. We sat on a fence by the pub*
>
> *PC. You knew exactly what the other two were doing didn't you?*
>
> *Sus. Yes.*
>
> *PC. So you stayed with the fruit as it was stolen – what keeping watch?*
>
> *Sus. I just stayed there – I wasn't going to go back and help.*
>
> *PC. If someone had come along and said something would you have warned the two stealing?*
>
> *Sus. Yes I suppose I would*
>
> *PC. So, as far as I can see you took part in the offence of shop lifting – yes?*
>
> *Sus. Yes*
>
> *PC. Then you sat willingly while the other two stole more stuff and you knew that they were stealing?*
>
> *Sus. Yes*
>
> *PC. And you say you were keeping watch?*
>
> *Sus. Yes but around the corner.*

The case file records that she had 'fully and frankly' admitted to shop-lifting although she had neither admitted to this offence nor even to being a 'look-out'. A similar ploy was used in relation to several cases of 'burglary' where juveniles claimed not to have been involved in the offence although they had been outside the premises at the time. Interviewers suggested that intentionally or inadvertently they must have acted as look outs.

McConville and Hodgson et al (1992) argue that admissions which are elicited as a result of directive questioning, including the use of leading and legal closure questions, are inherently more unreliable than those resulting from more neutral forms of questioning. This is because the questions the interviewer asks direct the suspect to particular answers rather than allowing him or her to provide an account in their own words. Interviews based on this form of questioning have a propensity to produce unreliable admissions irrespective of whether this is the result in individual cases.

The role of appropriate adult, social workers and solicitors

The PACE code of practice is clear about the role of the appropriate adult in interviews.

> 'Where the appropriate adult is present at an interview, he should be informed that he is not expected to act simply as an observer; and also that the purposes of his presence are, first, to advise the person being questioned and to observe whether or not the interview is being conducted properly and fairly, and, secondly, to facilitate communication with the person being questioned.' (PACE Codes of Practice 1991 C. para 11.16).

Parents or an appropriate adult, other than a social worker or solicitor, were present in interviews in around 80 per cent (131) of the cases in the sample. There was no evidence from the tape recordings that they were made aware of the PACE code of practice guidance on their role in the interview. There is no way of knowing, from the Evans and Ferguson (1991) data, whether appropriate adults were advised of this outside the formal interview.

Approximately three quarters (74.8 per cent N= 98) of the parents and appropriate adults who attended interviews made no contribution whatsoever. When parents did contribute they were as likely to be unsupportive (50.4 per cent N=66) as supportive of their children. An example of a supportive comment is a mother who, when her son is asked who has caused damage to a church, says that it is *'probably them that come on our estate and smash all our roofs'*. This is one a number of instances in which interviewing officers told parents to keep quiet.

In some cases parents try to explain to interviewing officers what their children are trying to say. In Case C/11/1 a boy had been arrested for being found on enclosed premises. During the interview it was suggested to him that the reason he had gone into the building was to steal a television. He denied this saying that they had just gone in to look around. His father intervened suggesting that

> 'Well, I get the impression that they were looking to see what was in there for a place to go, sort of secret and private. I mean, I can't condone what he has done, but I can sort of liken it to a den in a wood or something like that. But here you are in a city. I'm only suggesting that. I don't know. But that is what I think he is trying to say.'

When parents were unsupportive generally they either put pressure on their children to own up, told the police that they had washed their hands of them or that they should have known better. For example one father comments '*It's against the law, it's as simple as that. As a 16 year old he should have more sense*'.

Although parents are generally passive observers of their children's interviews they contribute substantially more than professionals. Solicitors attended interviews in approximately 11 per cent (18) of cases and in 9 of these the police used persuasive tactics and obtained a confession. Social workers, who were mainly residential social workers responsible for the care of the children being interviewed or specialist juvenile justice workers, attended interviews in approximately 18 per cent (29) of cases. In 18 of these cases the police used persuasive tactics and obtained a confession. There is only one example each of any contribution whatsoever from either of these professions. Again it is impossible to know from this data what advice might have been given outside the formal interview situation. But given the evidence that police questioning may exploit the interrogative suggestibility of suspects, professionals might have been expected to play a more interventionist role. They are either not aware of, ignore, or are unable or unwilling to assert themselves in order to ensure that the PACE code of practice which emphasise the potential vulnerability of juveniles is implemented (PACE Code of Practice 1991 Notes for guidance 11B).

Admissions, denials and disposals

As has been stated the analysis of the taped interviews included an assessment of whether the suspect had clearly admitted, clearly denied or made an admission that fell short of a full confession to the offence which was the subject of the interview. A central concern here is to see whether there are cases where there is a clear denial, or no clear admission, that are never-the-less dealt with by means of a caution. If there is no clear admission or a clear denial and the case goes to court then individuals have an opportunity to dispute police assertions about their guilt. Even here, however, there are risks since in practice defence solicitors or the Crown Prosecution Service rarely listen to tapes in order to verify police claims that suspects have made a full confession (Baldwin 1992). In addition confession evidence is rarely disputed in court so that even in these cases the police view of guilt is not effectively contested.

There was no attempt to enter into any complex legal judgements when making these assessments. In 13 cases the police record of the interview stated that the juvenile had made a full and frank admission but on a more detailed examination of the taped interview he or she had clearly denied the offence. Of these 13 cases 3 were prosecuted, 8 cautioned and 2 informally warned. In a further 5 cases the police record of the interview stated that the juvenile had made a full and frank admission but on a more detailed examination of the taped interview he or she had made an admission that fell short of a full confession. Of these 3 were prosecuted, 1 cautioned and no further action was taken with respect to the remaining case.

In 13 cases the police record of the interview contained no clear statement about whether the juvenile had made a full confession but on a more detailed examination of the taped interview he or she had clearly denied the offence. Of these 13 cases 3 were prosecuted, 3 cautioned, 3 informally warned and the remaining 2 cases were dealt with by means of no further action. In a further 7 cases the police record of the interview contained no clear statement about whether the juvenile had made a full confession and on a more detailed examination of the taped interview he or she had made an admission that fell short of a full confession. Of these 7 cases 3 were prosecuted, 1 cautioned and 3 informally warned.

In a total of 12.8 per cent (21) of cases in the sample of taped interviews therefore, suspects made clear denials or at least no clear admission during interviews, but were never-the-less either cautioned or informally warned. This represents 22.1 per cent of the cases that were disposed of by means of a caution or informal warning (N = 95). In 16 other cases juveniles were prosecuted when the police recorded that they had made a full and frank confession whereas they had in fact denied the offence or made an admission that fell short of a full confession. Reference has already been made in this study to one way in which this might come about. Interviewing officers may genuinely think that the suspect has made an admission and may record this on the case summary. Evans and Ferguson (1991) observed an example of this process when a case involving an alleged burglary was referred to a juvenile liaison panel for a decision about disposal. When a member of the panel challenged the admission evidence a closer examination of the interview transcript revealed that although the child admitted being in the building they had not admitted taking anything. They had not therefore admitted to a vital component of the offence of burglary. The crucial feature of this case is that this is one of the rare examples where the process of case review included a review of the content of the police interview. When cases are dealt with by means less than a prosecution case summary statements concerning admissions or denials are taken at face value. Evans and Ferguson (1991) report that in these circumstances it is very rare for anyone to listen to the taped interview once the interview is over and its corresponding case summary is completed.

The case described above is typical of cases in the sample of taped interviews. Juveniles admit being in buildings that they should not be in but deny taking anything. They admit taking things, in one instance a set of goal posts, but deny that they intended to keep them. They admit throwing stones, bricks, and in one instance a cherry stone, but deny that they were reckless or intended to break anything. They admit thinking that something they have bought might have been stolen, particularly when this is suggested to them in an interview, but deny knowing that it was. They admit doing something wrong but do not understand that they have committed an offence or deny it.

CONCLUSION

There have been various attempts to understand police interviews in terms of the chain of decisions which have to be made by interviewers and suspects (Irving and Hilgendorf 1980, Moston et al 1992). These decision making models may assume a higher degree of rationality in the interview process, on the part of both interviewers and suspects, than is often the case. The analysis of the sample of taped interviews used in this study suggests that police interviewers do not necessarily have a clear idea at the outset of the interview about how they are going to approach it. Similarly the responses of some juvenile suspects to questions suggest that they do not understand what is going on. They simply react situationally to the chain of events which they are enmeshed in rather than make rational decisions about whether or how they are going to answer questions.

This study makes no attempt to directly test the validity of decision making models of police interviews. This could be done, for example, by interviewing suspects and police officers about the basis for their decisions after the interview has been completed. The present study has, however, attempted to build on existing research in order to determine the factors affecting decisions to confess or deny offences during police interviews. These may be indicative of some of the main parameters of the decision making process.

The factor analysis

A key issue here is the extent to which police interview techniques determine the outcomes of interviews. There was no attempt to gather data about police interview techniques in the Evans and Ferguson (1991) research which is used as the basis for the factor analysis contained in the first part of this study. It is therefore not possible to directly assess the impact of interview techniques in the factor analysis. One measure, however, of the success of the use of persuasive interview techniques is whether or not suspects confess. According to the police records of the outcomes of interviews for the Evans and Ferguson (1991) case sample just over half of the juveniles (51.4 per cent) either denied the offence or made an admission that fell short of a full confession. One of the findings from the second part of the present study is that persuasive interview techniques were used in only a minority of cases (38 of the sample of 164

43

taped interviews) and resulted in a confession in only 19 cases. These findings suggest that the police used persuasive interview techniques resulting in a confession, in 19 of the 367 cases in the original Evans and Ferguson (1991) case sample. It follows that persuasive interview techniques were likely to have been an important, but relatively minor, factor determining whether or not the juveniles in the Evans and Ferguson (1991) sample confessed. Therefore the omission of this factor in the analysis contained in the first part of the present study is unlikely to significantly affect the results.

The factor analysis contained in the first part of this study suggests that four case characteristics have a bearing on the outcomes of interviews: strength of evidence, the criminal history of the suspect, the seriousness of the offence and the sub-division in which the interview takes place. Factors, which previous research suggests predispose suspect's to confess or deny their alleged offences, including age, sex, offence type and the presence or absence of a solicitor or social worker in the interview, were not statistically associated with interview outcomes. The factor analysis provides support for the view that police interview techniques and tactics have only a limited effect on admission rates (Irving and McKenzie 1989, Moston et al 1992). The finding that the outcomes of interviews are largely determined by legal variables stands in contrast to the wilder claims of supporters of the social construction of cases argument.

The interview process

The second part of this study is concerned to explore in more detail the interview process in those cases where the case summary records that suspects have fully admitted the offence or where it records no clear outcome. There are two important contexts for understanding the interview process.

First despite the 1981 Royal Commission on Criminal Procedure's desire to limit the use of the coercive power of arrest the opoosite appears to have happened. The arrest and detention of juveniles is a matter of routine (Evans and Ferguson 1991, McConville et al 1991). A significant number of juveniles are arrested when subsequently it is found that there is insufficient evidence to take action against them or that no crime has been committed. Thirty per cent (111) of the juveniles in the Evans and Ferguson (1991) sample were dealt with by means of no further action. In 71 cases this was because there was insufficient evidence and in a further 26 cases because the police decided that no crime had been committed. It is clear that a significant proportion of interviews with juveniles take place when it is subsequently found that there are little or no grounds for the 'reasonable suspicion' which is supposed to be a precondition of arrest.

That juveniles are arrested and interviewed when there is little or no evidence, or when no crime has been committed, has implications for the interview process. In these circumstances interviewers have little basis for conducting the interview. Listening to the sample of taped interviews confirms this. The formal interview should never be simply a fishing expedition as the police should have 'reasonable suspicion' prior to arrest. McConville and Hodgson et al (1992) conclude that when this occurs it is likely to result in the collapse of the interrogation or the resort to hostile questioning. The data from the taped interviews supports their conclusion.

The second context for understanding the conduct of police interviews with juveniles is that a significant number are arrested and interviewed in connection with very minor offences. Arguably if some of these had been committed by adults the police would have regarded them as 'rubbish' (McConville et al 1991) and not proceeded with them. The fact that the offences of many juvenile suspects are minor partially accounts for the finding that three quarters of the individuals in the sample of taped interviews readily admit to their alleged offence often in the first sentence or two of the interview. This in turn accounts for the fact that the majority of interviews in the sample are completed in under fifteen minutes and that the most frequent duration is a mere seven minutes. Most of these suspects appear to be ready and willing to own up to their offences perhaps safe in the knowledge that they are likely to be cautioned or informally warned.

In some cases there is irrefutable evidence that questioning has taken place prior to the formal interview and this is used as the basis for it. In others it is difficult to understand how suspects know what to own up to, in the absence of their being told what they are accused of, unless some discussion prior to the interview had taken place. Suspects are encouraged to make a clean breast of any other offences that they may have been involved in and to express remorse.

Some suspects readily confess even when there is no other evidence against them or the evidence is weak. This raises concerns about uncorroborated confession evidence and the possibility that they confess to gain release from an uncomfortable situation. In the interviews that could be described as perfunctory and routine the police use mainly simple information seeking questions. This finding is a clear refutation of McConville et al's (1991) assertion that the police *rarely* rely on this form of questioning.

It is perhaps not surprising that when suspects do not readily admit in interviews the police resort to the use of more persuasive tactics. They do this in approximately a quarter of the cases. The use of persuasive tactics is as likely to be unsuccessful in obtaining a confession as successful. This provides additional support for the view that police interviewing techniques and tactics are a relatively minor determinant of the outcomes of interviews There are only a small number of cases in which the police eventually obtain a confession when the suspect initially denies the offence and where the evidence is weak.

The use of techniques and tactics is a separate issue from the form of police questioning. McConville and Hodgson et al (1992) argue that particular types of questions are associated with unreliable confessions. These include leading and legal closure questions and there is evidence of their use in the sample of taped interviews. If it is true that confessions resulting from these types of questions are inherently more unreliable than those resulting from more neutral forms of questioning then it follows that the police ought to be encouraged to adopt a more information – gathering and less directive approach. This is particularly important in the case of juveniles who may be thought to be 'at risk' of being unwitting instruments of their own conviction because they do not understand the legal implications of police questions or their own answers.

For as long as the dominant mode of justice is adversarial it is likely that the police will continue to use persuasive interview techniques. Moston et al (1992) acknowledge that there are going to be cases in which their use is both legitimate and necessary. But they warn that in these cases *'the police will need to show that they did not behave oppressively and were aware of 'at risk' suspects'* (Moston et al 1992). The problem with the concept of 'oppressive questioning' is that, although it has a legal meaning, for example it is referred to in the Code of Practice of the Criminal Evidence Act 1984, there are few examples of oppressive questioning that have been established in court or been the subject of police disciplinary proceedings. Deciding what is oppressive is a matter of judgement and *'as much a philosophical issue as a legal one'* (Morris 1980).

By any standards there are examples of oppressive questioning in the sample of cases discussed here. On occasion juveniles are for example harangued, belittled or directly and indirectly threatened that they will not be left alone until the police either obtain irrefutable evidence or the suspect confesses. *'You don't want us to keep coming around do you?'*. If oppressive and persuasive tactics are used with juveniles, many of whom have committed minor offences, then this may be taken as an indication of their routine use in police interviews. The problem remains as to what constitutes *'legitimate persuasion'* and whether its use can be justified with groups, such as juveniles, who may be thought to be 'at risk' by virtue of their age.

If it is accepted that the interview is located in a system of adversarial justice, in which on occasion the police pit their wits against juveniles, then a potentially important ally is the appropriate adult. The the PACE code of practice acknowledges this in so far as it suggests that appropriate adults are not just there to observe but to advise and to ensure that the interview is conducted fairly. But by and large they leave juveniles exposed and unsupported. When parents contribute to interviews they are as likely to act for the police as for their children. This seems peculiarly inappropriate behaviour given the adversarial nature of the process. In addition the police may actively discourage parents from speaking in interviews.

It seems remarkable that professionals, who were privy to some of the exchanges documented here, appear either to ignore or to be unaware of their obligation to advise suspects and ensure that interviews are conducted fairly. This is more understandable with respect to social workers as their training is highly unlikely to equip them with a detailed knowledge of PACE or sufficient knowledge of the criminal justice system to enable them to advise or act for their clients in interviews.

Police records of the outcomes of interviews

A detailed examination of the taped interviews raises questions about the accuracy of the police record of the outcome of the interview in terms of confessions, admissions and denials. In some cases the police record of the interview stated that the suspect had made a confession and in others there was no clear statement about whether or not the suspect had confessed when in the researchers' judgement the suspect had clearly denied the offence. These cases may either be prosecuted or dealt with in other ways. Even when a case goes to court police claims that the suspect has made a full confession may not be verified as the Crown Prosecution Service or defence solicitors rarely listen to taped interviews. In approximately twenty per cent of cases that are cautioned or informally warned suspects clearly deny the offence or at least make no clear admission. According to Home Office guidance in force at the time of the research (Home Office Circular 14/1985) they should not have been dealt with in this way. This is perhaps not surprising given the extent to which the increased use of cautioning has involved a shift to 'administrative justice' (Pratt 1986).

Establishing proof of the building blocks of a legally sustainable case is clearly more complex than many police interviewers appear prepared to acknowledge. Indeed McConville et al (1991) recognise that establishing proof of states of mind such as intention and recklessness presents investigators and courts with '*a very difficult challenge achievable only by establishing circumstances so compelling that they lead to an irresistible inference that the accused must have intended or foreseen the forbidden consequences'*. In which case it should come as no surprise that on occasions interviewers readily accept admissions at face value.

The data in this study suggests that there are at least two sets of circumstances in which this is commonly problematic. In one set of circumstances the police interviewer leads the suspect through a set of questions designed to establish the legal components of the case. The overall logic of the set of propositions appears compelling to the suspects who may agree with them without understanding their legal implications. For example they may agree to a statement of the type 'so you knew that stealing it was wrong' even though they have not admitted to intending to keep whatever it is alleged they have stolen. In this set of circumstances suspects may appear to admit to the offence without accepting that they have done anything wrong. In essence they do not accept that they are guilty when an admission of guilt is a condition of a caution.

In the second set of circumstances the suspect accepts that they have done something wrong, for example entered a building when they should not have been there. They are therefore poised to accept that what they think they have done wrong is also a legal offence. So statements such as *'so you know that going into someone else's garden is wrong? (sic)'* is part of the process of persuading the suspect to accept and admit that they have committed a burglary if only because they were there at the time and did not take active steps to prevent it.

The point of these examples is not that they are clear cut, which they are not, but they are at least contestable. If these processes were located in an *'inquisitorial'* system of justice, which is primarily concerned to arrive at the 'truth', then they would be less problematic. As it is they are firmly located in an *'adversarial'* system where the job of the police is to construct a case for the prosecution (McConville et al 1991, Evans And Ferguson 1991). In practice, for those juveniles that are cautioned, the system is neither *'adversarial'* or *'inquisitorial'*. It is a system of *'summary'* justice where the fate of the defendant lies almost entirely in the hands of the police and the professional groups who contribute to inter-agency consultation. It is ironic that this can depend on the self-incriminating statements of suspects and their willingness to incriminate their 'mates'.

At the same time the policy of diversion poses dilemmas which appear difficult or impossible to resolve. The informality of the system is what enables juveniles to be dealt with quickly and in ways that are thought to be least stigmatising and least likely to lead to the development of criminal careers. Yet it is this very informality which encourages discretionary decision making and inadvertently leads to summary justice in some instances.

Policy implications

The continuing dominance of '*adversarial*' justice automatically places constraints on any easy technical fixes to the problems and dilemmas posed here in relation to the conduct of police interviews with juveniles. The following, however, are some general suggestions made on the basis of the findings from this study.

Clearly we need to know more about what, if anything, takes place prior to formal questioning. It is not clear at what point and in what terms juveniles are cautioned that what they say may be used in evidence against them. Even in formal interviews officers may need to be particularly careful, when cautioning juveniles, to ensure that they understand the full implications of what is being said to them. At present whilst interviewers appear to be meticulous in ensuring that suspects are formally cautioned this is routinised, formalised and generally perfunctory.

In a significant proportion of cases the suspects are not told what offence they are being questioned about or accused of. As researchers we have had difficulties in pinning down the exact nature of the charges made against some juveniles (Evans and Ferguson 1991) so it comes as no surprise to discover that some suspects simply do not understand why they are being interviewed. The interviewer(s) ought to be obliged to state clearly at the beginning of the interview the nature of the incident or the offence which they wish to question the suspect about.

It is not clear whether police officers receive any special training in interviewing 'at risk' suspects including juveniles. In general interview training material appears to apply to adults and juveniles alike. The evidence from this study suggests that training should be directed at ensuring that interviewers adopt a more information gathering and less manipulative approach to questioning. Training material might include specific examples of directive questions such as leading and legal closure questions. Interviewing officers may also need to be encouraged to go to greater lengths to ensure that juvenile suspects fully understand the legal implications and possible consequences of what they are agreeing with or stating they have done. It is acknowledged that persuasive interview tactics may be legitimate and necessary but the limits to their use should be clearly defined in policy and communicated in the training process.

The case review process should develop more stringent checks on the outcomes of interviews. One approach to this, currently in use in some forces, is to periodically randomly sample taped interviews and compare their contents to the case summary record of their outcomes.

PACE guidance on the appropriate adult needs to be implemented and police and social work training addressed to this issue. The police should be obliged to inform the appropriate adult of what is expected of them in the interview.

References

Baldwin, J. (1992). *The Conduct of Police Investigations: Records of Interview.* Royal Commission on Criminal Justice Research Study No. 2. London: HMSO.

Baldwin, J. and McConville, M. (1980). *Confessions in Crown Court Trials.* Royal Commission on Criminal Procedure. Research Study 5. London: HMSO.

Baldwin, J. and Bedward, J. (1991) 'Summarising tape recordings of police interviews'. *Criminal Law Review*, pp. 671–679.

Cahill, D. and Mingay, D. (1986). 'Leading questions and the police interview'. *Policing*, 2, pp. 212–224.

Durant, M. Thomas, M. and Wilcock, H. O (1972). *Crime, Criminals and the Law.* London: OPCS.

Evans, R. and Ferguson, T. (1991). *Comparing Different Juvenile Cautioning Systems in One Police Force Area.* Report to the Home Office Research and Planning Unit.

Evans, R. and Wilkinson, C. (1990). 'Variations in police cautioning policy and practice in England and Wales'. *The Howard Journal of Criminal Justice*, 29, 155–176.

Fitzmaurice, C. and Pease, K. (1986). *The Psychology of Judicial Sentencing.* London.

Gilbert, N. (1981). *Modelling Society: An Introduction to Loglinear Analysis for Social Researchers*, London: George Allen and Unwin.

Gudjonsson, G. and Clark, N. (1986). 'Suggestibility in police interrogation: a social psychological model'. *Social Behaviour*, 1, pp. 88–104.

Gudjonsson, G. and MacKeith, J. (1982). 'False confessions: psychological effects of interrogation'. In Trankell, A. (ed.) *Reconstructing the Past: The Role of Psychologists in Criminal Trials.* The Netherlands: Kluwer.

Gudjonsson, G. and MacKeith, J. (1988). 'Retracted confessions: legal, psychological and psychiatric aspects'. *Medicine, Science and the Law*, 28, pp. 187–194.

Holdaway, S. (1983). *Inside the British Police.* Oxford: Basil Blackwell.

Home Office. (1985). *The Cautioning of Offenders*. Home Office Circular 14/1985. London: HMSO.

Home Office. (1990). *The Cautioning of Offenders*. Home Office Circular 59/1990. London: HMSO.

Hood, R. (1972). *Sentencing the Motoring Offender*. London: Heinemann.

Irving, B. (1980). *Police Interrogation: A Case study of Current Practice*. Royal Commission on Criminal Procedure Research Study 2. London: HMSO.

Irving, B. and Hilgendorf, L. (1980). *Police Interrogation: the Psychological Approach*. Royal Commission on Criminal Procedure Research Study 1. London: HMSO.

Irving, B. and McKenzie, I. (1989). *Police Interrogation: The Effects of the Police and Criminal Evidence Act 1984*. London: The Police Foundation.

Laurie, P. (1970). *Scotland Yard*. Bodley Head

Leiken, L. (1970). 'Police interrogations in Colorado: The implementation of Miranda'. *Denver Law Journal*, pp. 471–53.

Leng, R., McConville M. and Sanders A. (1989). *Discretion to Charge and to Prosecute*. Report to the E.S.R.C.

Leng, R. (1992). *The Right of Silence in Police Interrogation: A Study of Some of the Issues Underlying the Debate*. Report to the Royal Commission on Criminal Justice.

Lewis, R. (1976). *A force for the Future: The Role of the Police in the Next Ten Years*. Temple-Smith, London.

Lipton, J. (1977) 'On the psychology of eyewitnesses testimony'. *Journal of Applied Psychology*, 62, pp. 90.

Lloyd-Bostock, S. and Shapland, J. (1986). 'The Police and Criminal Evidence Act 1984: some continuing questions for psychologists'. *Bulletin of the British Psychological Society*, 39, pp. 241.

Maguire, M. (1988). 'Effects of the PACE provisions on detention and questioning'. *British Journal of Criminology*, 28, pp. 19–43.

Mason, J. (1986). 'Expert evidence in the adversarial system of criminal justice'. *Medicine, Science and the Law*, 26, pp. 8.

Mawby, R. (1979). *Policing the City*, Farnborough, Saxon House.

McConville, M. and Baldwin, J. (1981). *Courts, Prosecution and Conviction*. Oxford: Clarendon Press.

McConvile, M., and Hodgson, J., with Jackson, M. and MacRae, E. (1992). *Custodial Legal Advice and the Right to Silence*. Report to the Royal Commission on Criminal Justice.

McConville, M., Sanders, A. and Leng, R. (1991). *The Case for the Prosecution: Police Suspects and the Construction of Criminality*. London: Routledge and Kegan Paul.

Mitchell, B. (1983). 'Confessions and police interrogation of suspects' *Criminal Law Review*, 1983, pp. 596–604.

Morris, P. (1980). *Police Interrogation: Review of Literature*, Royal Commission on Criminal Procedure Research Study 3. London: HMSO.

Morris, A. and Giller, H. (1987). *Understanding Juvenile Justice*. Beckenham: Croom Helm.

Moston, S., Stephenson, G. and Williamson, T. (1992). 'The effects of case characteristics on suspect behaviour during police questioning'. *British Journal of Criminology*, 32, pp. 23–40.

Moston, S. (1992 forthcoming) 'Police questioning techniques in Tape recorded interviews with criminal suspects'. *Policing and Society*.

Neubauer, D. (1974). 'Confessions in Prairie City: Some cause and effects'. *Journal of Criminal Law and Criminology*, 65, pp. 103–112.

Parker, H., Casburn, M. and Turnbull, D. (1981). *Receiving Juvenile Justice*. Oxford: Blackwell.

Parker, H., Sumner, M. and Jarvis, G. (1989). *Unmasking the Magistrates*. Milton Keynes: Open University Press.

Pease, K. (1988). *Judgements of Crime Seriousness: Evidence from the 1984 British Crime Survey*. Home Office Research and Planning Unit Paper 44. London: HMSO.

Pease, K., Ireson, J., Billingham, S. and Thorpe, J. (1976). 'The development of a scale of offence seriousness'. *International Journal of Criminology and Penology*, 5, pp. 17.

Powers, P., Andriks, J. and Loftus, E. (1979). 'Eyewitness accounts of females and males'. *Journal of Applied Psychology*, 64, pp. 339–347.

Pratt, J. (1986). 'Diversion from the juvenile court'. *British Journal of Criminology*, 26, pp. 212–33.

Pratt, J. (1989). 'Corporatism: the third model of juvenile justice'. *British Journal of Criminology*, 29, pp. 236–253.

Reiner, R. (1985). *The Politics of the Police*. Brighton: Wheatsheaf books.

Rossi, P. H., Waite, E., Bose, C.E., and Berk, R. E. (1974). 'The seriousness of crimes: normative structure and individual differences'. *American Sociology Review*, 39, pp. 224–237.

Samuels, A. (1989). 'Forensic evidence for the defence'. *Medicine, Science and the Law*, 29, pp. 293.

Sellin, T. and Wolfgang, M. (1964). *The Measurement of Delinquency*. New York: Wiley.

Softley, P. (1980). *Police Interrogation: An Observational Study in Four Police Stations*. Royal Commission on Criminal Procedure Research Study 4. London: HMSO.

Vennard, J. (1985). 'The outcome of contested trials'. In Moxon, D. (ed.) *Managing Criminal Justice*. London: HMSO.

Walker, M. (1978). 'Measuring the seriousness of crime'. *British Journal of Criminology*, 24, pp. 27–48.

Walker, N. (1971). 'Psychophysics and the recording angel.' *British Journal of Criminology*, 11, pp. 191–194.

Willis, C. (1988). *The Tape Recording of Police Interviews with Suspects*, Home Office Research Study 97. London: HMSO.

Printed in the United Kingdom for HMSO.
Dd.0297204, 1/93, C6, 3396/4, 5673, 221515.